Epic Cars

Porsche 911 GT3

JULIA GARSTECKI

BLACK
RABBIT
BOOKS

BOLT

Bolt is published by Black Rabbit Books
P.O. Box 3263, Mankato, Minnesota, 56002.
www.blackrabbitbooks.com
Copyright © 2020 Black Rabbit Books

Marysa Storm, editor; Catherine Cates,
interior designer; Grant Gould, cover designer;
Omay Ayres, photo researcher

Library of Congress Cataloging-in-Publication Data
Names: Garstecki, Julia, author.
Title: Porsche 911 GT3 / by Julia Garstecki.
Description: Mankato, Minnesota : Black Rabbit Books, [2020] | Series: Bolt.
Epic cars | Includes bibliographical references and index. | Audience: Ages 9-12. |
Audience: Grades 4 to 6.
Identifiers: LCCN 2018017952 (print) | LCCN 2018019261 (ebook) |
ISBN 9781680728484 (e-book) | ISBN 9781680728408 (library binding) |
ISBN 9781644660393 (paperback)
Subjects: LCSH: Porsche 911 automobile–Juvenile literature.
Classification: LCC TL215.P75 (ebook) | LCC TL215.P75 G37 2020 (print) |
DDC 629.222/2-dc23
LC record available at https://lccn.loc.gov/2018017952

Special thanks to McKinley Johnson for his help with this book.

Printed in the United States. 1/19

Image Credits
presskit.porsche.de:
Porsche Media Gallery, 23
(chassis); press.porsche.com:
Porsche Media Gallery, Cover (car),
4–5, 6, 8–9, 10–11, 12–13, 15, 16, 16–
17, 17, 19, 24, 24–25, 26, 26–27, 28–29;
rennlist.com: KA MOTORSPORT, 20–21;
Shutterstock: Elenamiv, Cover (bkgd); Jia Li,
31, Sam Moores, 3, 23 (bkgd), 32;
VanderWolf Images, 1
Every effort has been made to contact
copyright holders for material repro-
duced in this book. Any omissions
will be rectified in subsequent
printings if notice is given
to the publisher.

Contents

CHAPTER 1

Racing
Down the Road

The Porsche 911 GT3 roars
down the road. The small, sporty
car zips through curves. It speeds along
straightaways, blowing past other cars.
The car's appearance says **luxury**.
But the GT3 is all about power.

Porsche is pronounced por-SHUH.

Stylish and Speedy

Porsches are known for their good looks and speed. Porsche released the first 911 GT3 in 1999. The new 911 GT3 came out in 2017. Fans loved it. The little car thrilled drivers with its **acceleration**. They loved its big sound.

PARTS OF A 911 GT3

WING

REAR ENGINE

WHEELS

SMOOTH SHAPE

ROUND HEADLIGHTS

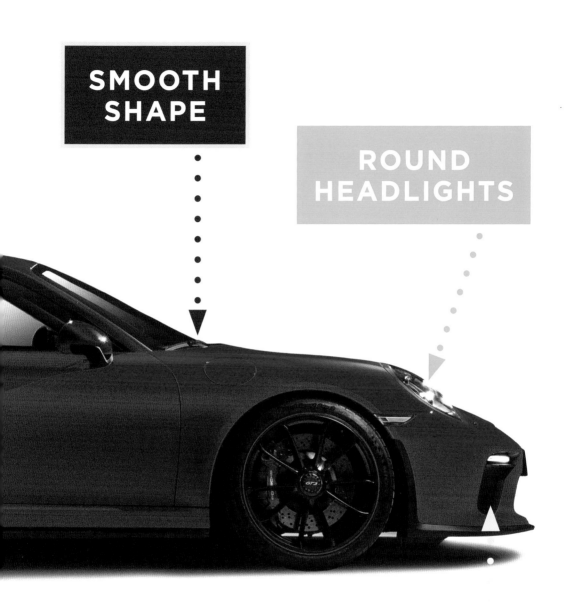

CHAPTER 2

Design

The GT3 is fast. Its top speed is almost 200 miles (322 kilometers) per hour. To increase the GT3's speed, designers used lightweight materials. Several parts are carbon fiber. The material is very light. But it's also strong.

Carbon fiber is about 10 times stronger than steel.

Quick and Cool

The car's light weight helps it reach high speeds. And its shape keeps it on the road. Designers made the GT3 to have **downforce**. The shape of the front and rear increases downforce. So do the wing and underbody panels.

The design helps keep the engine cool too. Large front vents take in air. That air moves to the radiators. Radiators cool the engine.

The 2017 GT3 has 20 percent more downforce than the previous GT3.

Simple and Clean

The GT3 has a simple leather interior. It comes with a touchscreen. The touchscreen shows information, such as average speed. The steering wheel doesn't have any buttons. Porsche left it plain so owners could focus on driving.

The GT3 has little soundproofing.
People inside can really hear the car roar.

MANY CHOICES

Buyers have many options when getting their GT3s.

15
EXTERIOR COLORS

4
WHEEL COLORS

5
SEAT BELT COLORS

3
SEAT OPTIONS

CHAPTER 3

Power and Performance

Beneath the GT3's hood lies a 4-liter 6-cylinder engine. It makes 500 metric horsepower. The GT3 can reach 60 miles (97 km) per hour in 3.2 seconds. With a manual **transmission**, the top speed is 198 miles (319 km) per hour.

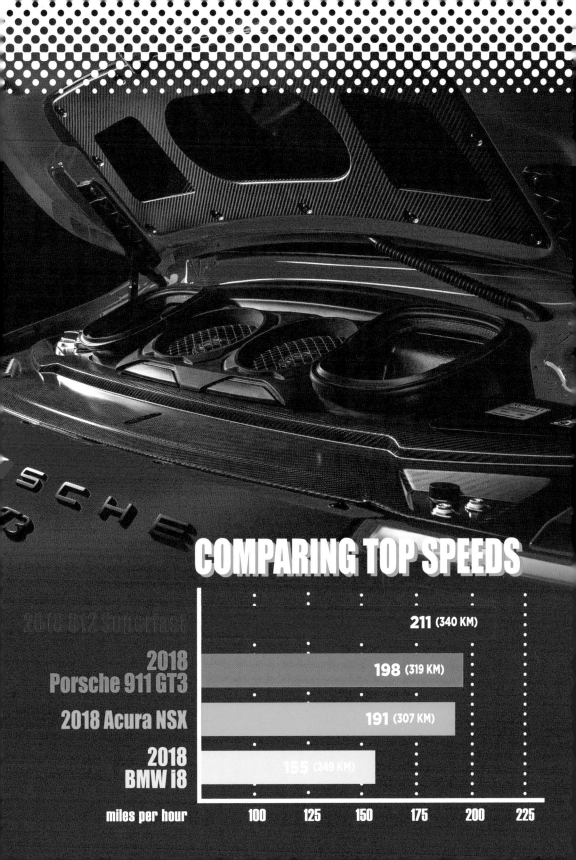

COMPARING TOP SPEEDS

	miles per hour
2018 D12 Superfast	211 (340 KM)
2018 Porsche 911 GT3	198 (319 KM)
2018 Acura NSX	191 (307 KM)
2018 BMW i8	155 (249 KM)

miles per hour: 100 125 150 175 200 225

Brakes

A fast car needs strong brakes. Buyers can get their GT3s with carbon-ceramic brakes. Like the rest of the car, they're light. But they're also strong. They help the driver control the car when slowing down.

Super Steering

The GT3 has rear-**axle** steering. At lower speeds, the back wheels don't turn with the front. They turn slightly in the opposite direction. This action improves **handling**. At higher speeds, the wheels turn the same direction. This action helps improve **stability**.

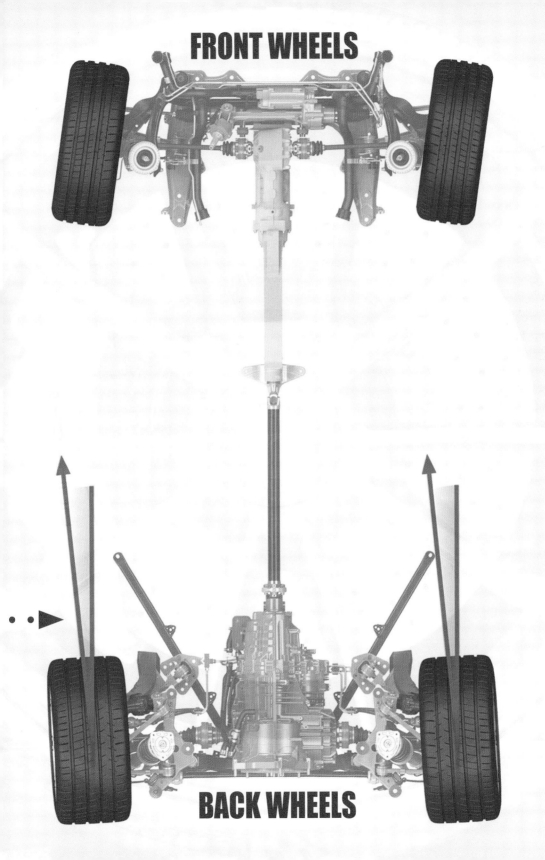

FRONT WHEELS

BACK WHEELS

911 GT3

TOP SPEED
198
MILES
(319 km) per hour

500
metric horsepower

3.2
SECONDS

TIME TO GO FROM
0 to 60 MILES
(97 KM) PER HOUR

911 GT3 RS

TOP SPEED
194
MILES
(312 km) per hour

520
metric horsepower

The GT3 RS

In 2018, Porsche showed off the RS version of the new GT3. RS stands for racing sport. The RS version has more horsepower. It has better cooling and more downforce too. The wheels are wider. They give the car more grip.

TIME TO GO FROM 0 to 60 MILES (97 KM) PER HOUR

3 SECONDS

By the Numbers

2
TOTAL SEATING

179.6
INCHES
(456.2 CM)
LENGTH

72.9
INCHES
(185.2 CENTIMETERS)
WIDTH
WITHOUT MIRRORS

ABOUT
$143,600
BASE PRICE

about
20
miles (32 km)
per gallon

ESTIMATED
HIGHWAY MILEAGE

CHAPTER 4

An

Porsche fans love the GT3. And the car will only get better. Future GT3s might have even lighter parts. A lighter GT3 would be even faster. The car might have bigger wings too. One thing is certain, GT3s will amaze drivers for years to come.

acceleration (ak-sel-uh-REY-shuhn)—the rate at which the speed of a moving object changes over time

axle (AX-uhl)—a fixed bar on which wheels spin

downforce (doun-FAWRS)—a force that increases the stability of a motor vehicle by pressing it downward

handling (HAND-ling)—the way a car, motorcycle, or other vehicle drives

luxury (LUHK-shuh-ree)—something that is expensive and not necessary

mileage (MAHY-lij)—the average number of miles a vehicle will travel on a gallon of gasoline

stability (stuh-BIL-i-tee)—being able to remain steady and stable

transmission (tranz-MI-shun)—a group of parts that takes energy from the engine to an axle that moves

BOOKS

Cockerham, Paul W. *Porsche: The Ultimate Speed Machine*. Speed Rules! Inside the World's Hottest Cars. Broomall, PA: Mason Crest, 2018.

Oachs, Emily Rose. *Porsche 911 Carrera*. Car Crazy. Minneapolis: Bellwether Media, Inc., 2018.

Piddock, Charles. *Porsche 911*. Vroom! Hot Cars. Vero Beach, FL: Rourke Educational Media, 2016.

WEBSITES

Porsche 911 GT3 / GT3 RS Reviews
www.caranddriver.com/porsche/911-gt3-gt3-rs

Porsche 911 GT3 Models
www.porsche.com/usa/models/911/911-gt3-models/

The new 911 GT3. Features.
www.youtube.com/watch?v=A4PB-BDOTe0

INDEX